MOURNING
SICKNESS

The Art of Grieving

KEITH SMITH

Resurrection Press
An Imprint of
CATHOLIC BOOK PUBLISHING CO.
Totowa • New Jersey

Revised Edition September 2003 by
Catholic Book Publishing/Resurrection Press
77 West End Road
Totowa, NJ 07512

ISBN 1-878718-85-1
Library of Congress Catalog Card Number: 2003108191

Cover design and photo by Keith Smith
Paintings by Keith Smith
Photographs of paintings by Tim Volk

Printed in the United States of America

1 2 3 4 5 6 7 8 9

This book is dedicated to the people who have helped.
They are the heroes in my life:

Debbie

Almira Rodriguez
Beverly Anello
Bill Moyers
Bob Cavalero
Carla and Dave Crockett
Carryl and Greg Hytopoulos
Emilie Cerar
Everyone at Commonweal
Ginny and Bill Truran
Ginny and Roland Johnson
Gloria Karpinsky
Gwen and Charles Dungy
Irene G. Smith
James T. Smith
Jean Erdman
Jim Gwynne
Joseph Campbell
Kathryn and Howard Perkins
Kathy and Nicolai Nielsen
Kelly and Doug Pellegrino
Kent J. Smith
Kim and Rob Holland
Leslie Appleton Young
Linda Samuels
Lori and Rich Harden
M. Scott Peck
Maria and Tony Lordi
Marielaine Mammon
Mary and Wink Dillaway
Michael Lerner
Michael Samuels
Naomi Remen
Robin and Steven Larsen
Sallie, Amie, Andy and Lynn Fasnacht
Sara and Arie Galles
Susan Chernak McElroy
Susan Lauter
Ula and Tim Volk
Wanda and Pat Loconto
Waz Thomas
and

Ginny, Talia and Chloe

CONTENTS

4

Introduction

Security is mostly an illusion. It does not exist in nature, nor do the children of humans as a whole experience it. Avoiding danger is no safer in the long run than outright exposure. Life is either a daring adventure or nothing. —Helen Keller

Helen Keller was both blind and deaf. Every step was a step into darkness; every move was a silent journey into the unknown. Whether we perceive it or not, the same is true for you and me. Our illusion of security and our imagined futures can be shattered by the smallest twist of fate. A car malfunctions, a cell in our body mutates, or we simply find ourselves in the wrong place at the wrong time. In small personal holocausts this illusion is unmasked every day.

Employer to employee:
"Your services are no longer needed."

Husband to wife:
"I do not love you anymore."

Doctor to mother:
"Your daughter was stillborn."

Oncologist to patient:
"You have cancer."

Police officer to parent:
"Your son has died in a car accident."

Tragedy happens constantly all around us and eventually it happens to us. There is no immunity from life. Life is hard and the occurrence of death within your life renders it even harder. Death is inconvenient; it comes at the wrong time and in the wrong place, and it happens to all the wrong people. Death lacks discrimination. It is blind. It takes babies and gangsters, saints and sinners. It is not fair. No amount of complaining, pleading, or praying makes it go away. It just is. We can ignore it; we can disguise it; we can pretend it does not exist; but the reaper always comes and Charon the ferryman takes the coins from our eyes and we suddenly see life, as it is, both wonderful and horrible. Life is not designed for our comfort and ease. Life is our teacher, and we have been placed here to learn. What follows is what I learned.

This book begins with the death of my wife. Debbie died from aplastic anemia which developed into acute leukemia. She was thirty-seven years old. We were living in a SoHo loft in New York City at the time of her diagnosis. Debbie was a Vice President at the World Headquarters of the Chase Manhattan Bank, and I am an artist and a college professor. Deborah's diagnosis was terminal and she was given two to six months to live by doctors at two of the best teaching hospitals in the nation. There was no conventional treatment for her condition, which was a complete failure of the bone marrow. Her body stopped producing blood and her immune system was all but nonexistent. She lived for seventeen months. She was a powerful intellect and spirit and was determined to fight for her life. We investigated every manner of alternative medicine: diet, herbs, yoga, visualization, meditation, hypnosis and healers. In the end she died a slow, painful death. She weighed 87 pounds.

In all of our searching we found no cure for her body, but we did find healing and peace from a one-week retreat called the Commonweal Cancer Help Program. The program was part of the Bill Moyers PBS series entitled *Healing and the Mind.* That week changed our lives. We walked on the beach, ate good food, practiced yoga, were massaged, wrote poetry, but most of all talked in the deepest most real way to people who had gone through or were going through the experience of severe illness with a heightened awareness of their mortality.

Following Debbie's death I had a succession of vivid and illuminating dreams. The information delivered in these dreams spoke of life after life and a new direction in my life. I had not painted for the two years during her illness, and suddenly in dreams I was not only told to paint but specifically what to paint. I felt compelled to read certain books and I began to write, in an automatic way, letters, poems, stories and my dreams. All of this creativity was occurring at the absolute lowest time of my life. I cried constantly and I felt emotionally gutted, but strangely it was also a period of sweet grace for me.

The paintings, poems, stories and dreams in *Mourning Sickness* chronicle the gestation period of grief and also describe the birth of a larger life, a wider love and the reopening of my heart. I offer this book to those who have experienced profound loss and seek to find meaning and beauty in life once again.

Keith Smith

THE SILENT SERMON
Black and white oil paint on canvas   48″ x 72″

🏵 1 🏵
DREAMS

Debbie died at two fifteen in the afternoon on February nineteenth. The night after her death, I had the most extraordinary and vivid dream. I was in a hospital being restrained by three doctors. They were pleading with me not to go into Debbie's room. They said her body had decomposed, and if I saw her in that condition, it would leave me with a very unpleasant final vision. I became angry and pushed them aside and told them I had to see her. I ran to her room and opened the door. Debbie was reclining, unclothed, on her side, in the way of the Odalisque in the painting by Ingres. Her body was radiant, full and perfect. Her hair shined like golden threads and her lips and cheeks were pink and glowing. I stared at her in amazement. The doctors were wrong. She had become perfect. I went to her bedside and sat down. Her eyes were closed, and her limbs hung limp. I put my arms around her and as I did, her chest heaved, her eyes and mouth opened and her lungs filled with air. My heart soared and my eyes welled with tears of joy. Debbie looked up at me and said, "Keith, I am not alive."

My heart descended as quickly as it had taken off. I thought, how could this be, she's not alive and yet I am holding her in my arms; she's dead and I'm talking to her. Then my mind slowly embraced the idea that this was a visitation from a place beyond the grave. In contrast to my waking life, in my dream I had no resistance to this concept. I paused and then asked her, "Is it good or bad where you are?"

She looked at me and rolled her eyes in the way she would when I had said something really dumb and then replied, "Good and bad do not apply here."

I said, "Well, is it okay, are you okay?"

Debbie's lips tightened and her eyes squinted as if to say, let me think about that one. Then slowly she nodded her head and said, "Yes, it's okay, it will take some getting used to, but it is okay."

I held her shoulders and looked into her face and asked, "When I die, will I be able to be with you?"

She said, "Yes."

Her eyes then closed and her body went limp again. I panicked and ran into the corridor and began a desperate search for the doctors. The halls were deserted. I decided to go back to Debbie's room, but I could not find my way. I began opening the doors in the corridor, but all the rooms were empty. I awoke sitting upright in bed half expecting her to be lying next to me.

On March fifth, Debbie came to me again in a dream. We were standing at the bottom of a large square stairwell. The stairs wrapped around the four walls of the well and extended upward for such a distance that I could not see the end. Debbie was wearing a hospital gown and was very thin and frail as she was in the last months before her death. During those months Debbie needed my help to walk and had fallen on two occasions when she had attempted to move unaided.

In the dream she began to walk up the stairs, and I immediately said, "Wait, let me help you."

Debbie turned to me and said, "Keith, I don't need your help anymore." I said, "Well, be very careful, I don't want you to hurt yourself."

In a very determined voice she spoke, "I don't have to be careful anymore. I'll show you." She not only continued to climb the stairs, but to climb onto the banister and dance and leap like a gymnast on a balance beam. Up the stairwell she went with amazing grace and fluidity, never stopping to look where her foot would step next. So quickly she flew that, though I ran my fastest, I could not keep up, and soon she was out of my sight and many flights ahead of me. Suddenly I heard her fall. I tore up the stairs taking two and three steps at a time. When I came upon her she was reclining on the banister.

I said, "Are you all right?"

She answered, "Yes, I'm fine."

I said, "Won't you be bruised from the fall?"

She said, "Nothing can hurt me now."

I embraced her and she looked up at me and said, "Keith, wake up."

Again, I sat straight up in bed and I was a thousand-cups-of-coffee awake. My heart was like a giant fist pounding on my rib cage. I tried to regulate my breathing. I looked at the clock. It was one thirty-eight in the morning. I had fallen asleep with the television on and as my eyes adjusted to the light of the screen I saw and heard Bill Moyers interviewing Joseph Campbell. The program was entitled "The Message of the Myth" from a series of interviews called *The Power of Myth*. The particular message being delivered at that moment was so appropriate, life affirming, and comforting to me that I was tempted to believe Debbie had wakened me so I could hear it.

My ability to believe that Debbie could contact me and deliver messages from beyond the grave was tempered by the fact that nearly everything that I experienced since her death seemed filled with meaning and message directly from her. The way a bird would come to the window and look in at me, the way a plant would break the surface of the earth and heliotrope to face the sun and the coming spring, the words of a song on the radio seemed to say to me . . . "Hold on for one more day."

I asked myself, "Can everything be significant?"

As powerful as these waking voices seemed none were as potent as my dreams. These were nothing like the misty vellum images that came to me in a normal night's sleep. These dreams felt absolutely real with all of my senses engaged.

Upon awakening I truly felt as though I had touched and talked with Debbie.

Four nights passed. Early in the morning I had another dream. Debbie and I were standing at the end of a long serpentine road. Debbie was radiant, full of light, and wearing a flowing white robe. She seemed more spirit-like and less physical than she had in my other dreams. The road before us was made up of multi-colored flagstones, purple, gray, green and terra cotta red. The road was in disrepair. Grout between the stones was missing and the stones were cracked and uneven. In the far distance, a road crew was working very hard at laying a new, wider and longer highway on top of the old flagstone road. They were shoveling a reddish-brown asphalt onto the road, and a steamroller followed them compressing and smoothing the surface. I held Debbie's hand and looked at her and said, "The new highway isn't as beautiful as the old road."

She said "No it isn't, but it will be smooth and it will serve you well. It's up to you to make it beautiful."

I replied, "Can't we fix the old road?" She said, "No, it's too far gone to repair."

Debbie then said to me, "Wake up now Keith." Again, I awoke breathless, pulse pounding and with the television on. It was around five a.m., and there was Joseph Campbell speaking the exact same message to me at the exact same moment in the interview. The program was being rebroadcast during the early morning hours to allow schools to tape the show. The message being delivered was about God. It was powerful and beautiful, and I believe Debbie was telling me: THIS is the way it is. I have always been a little thick about grasping spiritual things, so I think she knew that I needed to view a rebroadcasting of her message as well.

The view of God and the world that Joseph Campbell described was one he had found repeatedly in the heart of many myths, from various cultures and in the soul depths of the great religions. A perennial philosophy, a single thread ran through the labyrinth of spiritual beliefs. This thread leads to a much larger vision of God and the world than I had ever conceived. In fact it was a God beyond our powers of conception but well within our powers of perception.

God, my vision of God, my Mighty Fortress of a God, had failed me. I was outside of that fortress and shielded from his love. God, my childish Santa Claus gift-giving genie in the bottle, wish-granting, prayer-answering, miracle-performing God, had failed me. It seemed I was unworthy of the miracles he doled out so casually two thousand years ago.

During Debbie's illness and pain I would fall on my knees and beg God for help, for a cure. I would bargain with God, "Make her well and I will give all of our money to the poor; cure her cancer and I will try to be perfect; let her live and take me instead." I carried a roll of dollar bills in my pocket and gave them to street people and the homeless in the hope that if I were kind enough and good enough, God might answer my prayers. In the final hours my prayers were for an end to Debbie's pain. That prayer was answered.

I felt contempt for the Sistine God I had grown up with, the white maned, white skinned, eighty-year-old, flying body builder. He who points his lifegiving, accusing finger at poor Adam frescoed on the Vatican chapel ceiling. Adam reclines with a suspicious and worried look. He tenuously half extends his index finger toward the pumped up octogenarian. If God had introduced himself to me at that time, it would have been the middle digit of my hand that I extended to him.

My belly was fired with anger and hate. The state of hate is hard to live in. It is not a united state; in fact, it separates you from everyone and everything. God was not flawed, but my vision of God was. Life was not a mistake, but my understanding of life was mistaken. I needed a new vision of the eternal, of God. Debbie's dream visitations turned me away from anger and pointed me toward healing, acceptance and ultimately, love.

Memorial services were held for Debbie on both coasts. We let a flock of white balloons fly out over a lake in New Jersey and out over the Pacific in California. Dear friends spoke, and after each service I was shocked by the number of people, mostly women, who told me they had dreamed about Debbie or had somehow felt her presence. Michael Lerner is the founder of a wonderful healing place called Commonweal. Debbie and I had attended the Cancer Help Program at Commonweal. Our experience in that program was one of profound healing. During our stay there Michael and Debbie made a pact that if she died she would make an attempt to contact him. When I called to inform him of her death he immediately asked what time she had died. I told him the time of death and he said that he had felt her presence that day and at that time.

A month after the memorial I received a message on my answering machine from Waz Thomas, the director of Commonweal, saying, "Keith, this is Waz. I have a message for you from Debbie, please call me." I called Waz at Commonweal, and he told me that on the first of April he had driven from San Francisco to his home in Bolinas, California. He parked in the driveway next to his house, and as was his habit before getting out of his truck, he settled into a meditation focusing his attention on the trees and flowers on his front lawn.

He said suddenly he was aware that Debbie was there with him and that she was light and fluid and dwelling in a comfortable space. Then she spoke to him and said, "I want you to deliver a message to Keith. Tell him to start painting. His new paintings are going to be important, and I want to see them."

I am an artist and an art professor and I have painted continuously since I was a boy, but during Debbie's illness I had been unable to paint and since her death, I feared painting. I feared that all I felt, all I had to express was anger and pain. I was living in pain. Why, for God's sake, would I want to paint pain? When Debbie was alive, and I had slipped into lethargy, she would sweetly urge me into action by saying, "Smitty you bum! Get your butt in gear." That day I felt as though I had received a long distance kick to my fanny. I began painting that afternoon.

I had not worked in my studio for two years. The first painting I completed is on the cover of this book. It absorbed many tears. That painting and all the paintings that followed it were done in black and white because I could find no color in my life. When I was stuck and wanted to stop painting, Debbie would come to me as she did when she was alive and urge me on. The second painting I finished depicts an empty bed with an absent figure impressed in the sheets and pillow. In the autumn before her death Debbie had planted columbine seeds near the front door of our house. In early spring they surfaced and quickly formed sorrowful little buds that bowed their heads and wept the dew. In late spring these sad pilgrims blossomed, their pastel faces tilted to the sun. They threw back their crowned heads in triumph over the long, dark winter. I saw despair and hope in these flowers and felt compelled to add the image to the painting of the empty bed.

A journal entry from that time reads:

Debbie has not spoken to me for a while now, except when I cry at night I have felt her reach down and kiss my face on the cheeks and forehead, in the way she would kiss me every morning after I shaved. I ache for her and feel so utterly alone, and yet there is also a growing acceptance of the road that lies before me.

Can everything be significant?

THE FLOWERBED
Black and white oil paint on canvas   84" x 60"

❧ 2 ❧

HALLOWED BE THY NAME

When someone you love deeply, someone whose life is enmeshed with your own dies—a strange thing happens—time stops. The future you envisioned with that person is shattered. It forces you to realize, possibly for the first time, that your future plans are just that; plans, merely ideas, not tangible realities. This is why I believe every death of a significant other (child, spouse, lover, parent, dear friend) is a sudden death. Future hopes and plans are the final illusion to dissolve when we stand before the spiritless body of a loved one. No greater proof of the existence of a soul is needed after you have watched life leave the body of your beloved. The bargaining talk with God changes from: "Please God, take me, not them," to "Please God, take me also." When we say, "I cannot believe they are gone," the "they" we talk about is not only the loved one, but also the life plans we made, the second honeymoon, the camping trip, a child's graduation, marriage and so on.

A physical sensation of numbness occurs, the result of shock. Your future gone, standing in the present moment, you are as close to seeing the world as it really is as you can be on this side of death.

The next shock is... the world continues.

Well-meaning people say to you things like, "time will heal," when for you time has ceased to exist. They say, "You are young, you can marry again," or "You can have another child," as though the missing presence of your beloved was a broken part that merely needs replacing. They want you to get better fast, for when they see your pain, your loss, it shakes the foundation of their own imagined futures. These people are not evil or even stupid, they are simply uninitiated and why should their worlds stop to take account of your grief?

I remember walking in the spring after Debbie's death and being amazed that crocus, tulips and daffodils could still bloom. It was like the old Brenda Lee song, "Why do the birds go on singing? Why do these eyes of mine cry? Don't they know it's the end of the world? It ended when you said good bye."

The answer is yes, the world knows death very well. It is we who are unacquainted with it. The griever is in fact hyper-aware of loss and the cycles of existence. The wilting flower, the road-killed cat, a friend's divorce, all are participants in this fantastic, horrific dance of birth, life and death, and you see it as you have never seen it before. You are in the midst of the dance, mourning but also giving birth to a new self, and, like any birth, it is painful.

You are the ultimate dispassionate observer because you are just that, without passion. It is hard to believe a person can exist with a large hole in the middle of his or her chest. It is a strange but universal sensation called a "broken heart" and yet that does not fully describe the feeling. It is not on the left side of the chest, but dead center, and the words "dead center" do describe it. It is bigger than a missing heart. It is the feeling of being gutted, hollowed, or perhaps I should say, hallowed.

The word hallowed means to make holy. You are futureless, without the illusion of a future, passionless, numb, neither feeling love nor hate and living in the present moment, super aware of the here and now. This is the state Zen Masters, Yogis and mystics from many faiths practice for years to achieve. Although you are anxious to leave it behind, there are things to be learned here. The following is a very old story that has been told and written many times.

The Cup

A college professor visited the Zen Master. The professor told the Master he wanted to learn about Zen. The professor proceeded to tell the Master about himself, his theories, his dreams, and his plans for the future. The Master listened quietly and then served tea. He filled the professor's cup and continued to pour until it overflowed. The professor said, "Stop, stop, it is full, no more will go in!" The Zen Master said, "Like the cup you are full of your opinions and speculations. How can I teach you unless you first empty . . . (make hollow) your cup?"

Inside Information

do not tell me
time will heal
my future is gone
my heart just feels
broken
do not tell me
new love will come
when all i sense
is aching numb
emptiness
while true
all your words may
be
this knowledge must grow
from inside of
me

Honed Stone

a squadron
of pelicans
fly
in formation
above my head
their shadows
momentarily
block the sun
as i slowly walk the beach edge
where dark wet sand arcs into
dry light
where waves
deposit
the ocean leftovers
bit of kelp
piece of shell
once jagged stone
honed to a smooth disc

Oh God
smooth
the burrs
of bitterness
off my soul
burnish the fear
from my heart
polish the edges
of my anger
make me
the glistening smooth stone
that feels good in your hand
take me home
and place me on your mantle

HOPE
Oil paint on oak panel   18″ x 32″

❧ 3 ❧
THE KEEPING OF THE SOUL

The modern American rituals for death and grief are efficient but inadequate. We place the body in a box, or if the body is displayed it is made to look as alive as possible. Eyes closed, in repose, laid to rest, our language and our senses are asked to view the body as asleep. This obscures and diffuses the great lesson to be learned from death. The lesson is that we are not our bodies, but that our bodies are the vehicles of our consciousness. By denying death of the body we weaken the wonder of our soul's existence. The soul's sustenance is the power point of life.

The Native American tribe called the Ogalala Sioux have a ritual that honors the presence of the soul, nurtures the mourning survivor and supports a vision of people, animals, plants, earth, sky and spirit as being connected and in reality, one. This belief has been substantiated by the discovery of subatomic particles, which are the building blocks of all matter. The ritual is called, "The Keeping of the Soul."

> The beloved of a person who has died seeks the counsel of the tribal priest. The priest instructs the mourning survivor, "Your loved one's body is dead, but their soul is here with us even now. We must care for this soul while it is dwelling with us. You who loved this person more than any other shall be the keeper of the soul."

> There is a prayer ceremony held just after the death of the beloved. The body of the deceased is placed high on a wooden scaffold. Halfway between heaven and earth, the body is offered to all the elements. It will become part of the sky through the birds. It will become part of the earth through the animals, insects and plants. This is

24

good, for this body was sustained by all of these creatures during its life. A lock of hair is taken from the deceased and placed in a pouch. The lock of hair is tied with buckskin and is considered a holy representation of the loved one's soul.

The Keeper of the Soul is told to make themselves holy in thought, word and deed. The Keeper is not allowed to work or cook for their sole job is to honor and remember their beloved, to grieve with great intensity and dignity. The people of the community are instructed about the importance of this job and their role in supporting the Keeper. Having and holding one of holy purpose strengthens them all. The Keeper does this mourning work until ready to let the soul go. The Keeper of the Soul alone decides when this will be. At the time of release another prayer ceremony is held where there is crying and grieving, but also joy. The soul is released, grief is honored and life affirmed.

When you have lost someone you love, it is both your job and your duty to grieve. Your tears remind those around you that life is temporal, temporary, involved with time; that love is persistent, ongoing, even after death; that the soul is eternal, not involved with time, existing in the now of every shining moment.

Blessed are those who mourn, for they will be comforted.
Matthew 5:4

The Drowning Survivor

a gossamer gauze
of sight, time and mind
obscures my vision
of the sublime
i see the contour softly
silhouetted in a mist
i reach out too hardly
from murky water's depths
diamond net reflect my soul
lift me up so i can know
the shimmering lace
working light
that bridges all
the burning life
Great Spirit
help me to make
my intentions pure
let me touch
the you in me
the part that will
endure

The Drowning Survivor
Black and white oil paint on canvas   48″ x 32″

❦ 4 ❦

HABEAS CORPUS

Habeas corpus is a Latin term meaning: The body should be here. A writ of *Habeas corpus* issued by a judge is an order to produce the living, breathing body, that is the person at issue. I think almost anyone who has lost a loved one longs to write such a writ. All this talk of heaven, soul, spirit and dreams does not bring back the physical presence of your beloved and that is what the grieving survivor truly desires.

I can remember as a boy reading a comic book in which Superman flew at high speed against the earth's rotation and by doing so reversed time and proceeded to change history and prevent Lois Lane's death. What would life be like if we had the power to undo death? Think it through. What a silly, meaningless, crowded world it would be without death, without endings. Who would read a biography that went on and on; who would listen to music with no finale; sex without love very quickly becomes exercise, what would it be without a climax and dinner, a continuous presentation of entrees with no dessert? Imagine the hell life on earth would be if everyone who had ever lived was still alive and still here among us. Procreation would be illegal. The rationing of food and space would be a necessity. Maybe life on earth is not flawed. Perhaps God knows what he's doing, or if you do not believe in God then possibly the processes of nature and evolution are all working, as they should.

Of course when I wished for the power to overrule the laws of physics, turn back time and raise the dead, I did not want everyone to have that power. I only desired it for me and those I love.

Hubris is a kind of super arrogance where a human being believes himself to be equal to or better than God. I engaged in a kind of hubris by constantly asking God the childish question, "Why?"

Whying

why her
why not me
why not the
wino
passed out in the street
why no
miracles
why no
answered prayers
father
why hast thou forsaken me
in my moment of despair
God helped me pass a test
God helped me land a job
i know now i did those things
without my prayers to God
the God spirit that is inside me
and in all matter too
evolution and survival
these are God's gifts to you
life itself is your miracle
free will
your answered prayer
give thanks for these
when you are whying
and you're sure that
God's not there

❧ 5 ☙
POSTCARDS FROM HEAVEN

I believe that dying is God's way, the world's way, life's way of telling you your work here is done. Most resist, some accept and others are anxious to move on. No one is too young, too good, too smart or too beautiful to die. We are told that Jesus was a perfect human who lived a sinless life and yet he was delivered to eternity through a painful and humiliating death. A death he asked God if he could avoid.

"Father, if you are willing, remove this cup from me"
Luke 22:42

God said no to Jesus and God says no to us. In the end Jesus and all of us must face our common fate. However, I do not believe that death means God is finished with you. I do believe when you die God gives you new work to do, a promotion, a raise and a chance to see the world (as it really is). This means you will be out of physical contact with the people you love but not out of spiritual contact. Like postcards from heaven, the loved ones you leave behind can receive your dreams and your visions, but most of all they hold the memory of you as if welded to their hearts. You are a part of them and can truly never be apart from them.

When Jesus was aware of his coming death he asked his friends to remember him, his body, his blood, his life with them, whenever they ate a piece of bread or drank a glass of wine. He wanted to be part of their hearts. When you remember a song, a place or a face shared with your beloved, you perform a sacrament that reminds you of the part of your heart that is them.

communion   *1. a sharing; possession in common; 2. a sharing of one's thoughts and emotions; 3. a close relationship with deep understanding; 4. a religious or holy body; 5. a sharing in or celebrating of The Holy Eucharist*

TO: *Heaven*
FROM: *Earth*

Dearest_____,

I miss you and wish you were here.
I hope you are adjusting to your new job.
Are you enjoying seeing the world?
I look forward to a time when we will be together again,
but I still have work to do here on Earth.
I think of you every day.

Love,

_____

31

The Shock of the Old
Black and white watercolor on rag paper   12″ x 9″

The Shock of the Old

the shock of the old
when naked and trembling
truth is told
that ancient nature
to you applies
winged wisdom takes
you by surprise
pierced by thorny talons
lifted by the claw
you soar above the carrion self
and see what others saw
through God's eye you glimpse
as a life slowly ebbs
your little place
in eternity's web

❧ 6 ❧
HOLIDAYS AND HOLY DAYS

I have great neighbors. A few days before Debbie's last Christmas a group of about twenty of the sweet people who live nearby gathered together. It was the snowiest and coldest night of the year. With flashlights in hands they came shivering to the front of our house, singing, "Joy To The World!" Debbie came down from our bed and knelt on a chair in the living room and looked out at the love through the frosted glass. They sang their entire repertoire in fifteen minutes and then we invited the blue-lipped choir into the house. Almira, Debbie's mother served hot apple cider to warm their bodies as they had warmed our souls.

One year later I was sitting alone in that living room crying. No tree, no lights, no joy to the world. Holidays had become terrible reminders of all that was missing in my life. I wept like a baby at my sister-in-law's wedding. I gave no thanks at Thanksgiving. I dreaded Christmas and wanted only to have a silent night. But that early December evening I was invited to dinner at Pat and Wanda's, my good neighbors on the south side of Rainbow Trail. Ginny and Bill, my good neighbors to the north side, were also invited.

I took a deep breath, put on a happy face and walked into their home. It was beautifully decorated. The five of us sat around the dinner table and a sixth empty chair reminded me that she was not there. But in a way she was there, for Pat and Wanda had placed a plate with napkin, silverware and goblet where she would have sat. Then Pat did a remarkable thing. He lifted his glass and said, "Here's to Debbie." All at the table repeated, "To Debbie." A tear traced a line from my eye to my chin. Pat then told of how he had lost his best friend at a young age. He asked if I minded if we toasted again. I said, "Certainly not, I'm sure they are both near, and it is a great relief to speak of my grief with my friends."

A strange thing happens about six months after your beloved's death; people stop speaking their name. They stop referencing them in their conversation with you. It is a subtle conspiracy aimed at making themselves more comfortable in dealing with you. When you persist in mentioning your loved one, you will find that chance meetings end quickly, conversations abruptly stop and people find an arsenal of excuses to use in getting themselves as far away from you as possible. I let them go. My neighbors, my friends put their personal comfort aside and gave me a great present that evening. They spoke Debbie's name out loud ten months after her death. It was the sweetest sound.

It makes you crazy
to try to be happy
when you are sad
when you feel awful
and pretend to be glad
true friends will let you be you
to feel what you feel and do what you do
do not let ANYONE tell you how you should feel
Your feelings are yours your emotions are real
and giving voice to your pain can help you to heal
It was then I decided
that Debbie would be part of the holidays that year
and for me these would be holy days of sadness and tears
i would talk about her and how i felt inside
i could not pretend that she had not died
that year the presents i gave were from Debbie and Keith
two packages marked Christmas joy and Christmas grief

❦. 7 ❦

REVIEWING THE OPTIONS

So you are in pain; you have a black hole in your chest; you cry constantly; no one understands you, and I tell you it's your duty to grieve.

What is this poop anyway! He not only points out I have been served a big bowl of it, but he wants me to call it ice cream. Well, screw you Mr. pompous know-it-all Keith Smith. Screw all of you who sent me cards and dropped off cakes but now don't call me because I have a bad attitude and I depress you, and screw all of you who do call and ask me how I am and when I don't say fine or okay want to get off the phone as quickly as possible and while we are at it, screw you _____ (insert name of deceased beloved) for leaving me with all of these problems and SCREW YOU _____ (insert name of deity or supreme being) for creating a world with all this crap in it. Oh no, I just told God to get screwed; now I'm going to get it. So what? What could God do to me that is worse than this ?

(See Old Testament, Book of Job)

Life is fully capable of dealing you worse events than those you are currently occupied with. You could be disabled; someone else you love could die; you could get cancer. Don't you love it when people tell you about things that are more awful than the thing you are going through so that you will feel better? This works about as well as when mothers try to get their kids to eat their peas because children are starving in Ethiopia.

Gee, I was thinking the world was just awful, now I can see that it's really horrible. Thanks for straightening me out; I think I'll go kill myself now.

Uh oh, I said . . .

Kill Myself

I considered this option. One of the reasons I chose not to exercise this option was because I was angry with God. I said to God, "How could you kill my wife and put me through this grief?" Is the answer to kill myself and put everyone who loves me through grief also and then they could all kill themselves and soon everyone would be dead and, boy, we would have taught God a lesson then.

Killing yourself is the option without options. If you do it right, you do not have the option of saying, "Well I'm dead now, this really sucks, I'm going back and resume my grief." Perhaps you do have that option if you believe in reincarnation, but according to the rules of karma you will end up in the same place, back here on earth studying Remedial Grief or Grief 101. If you believe that when you die you are just gone, remember you are just guessing, and you could end up in a place worse than you are now.

> Grief World: (a planned community for those who killed themselves to escape grief on earth) around-the-clock bereavement groups, funerals three times a day, and the daily newspaper only prints obituaries.

I hope I have talked you out of killing yourself. If you continue to feel hopeless seek out help. Go to your priest; see your doctor; talk to your family and friends. Life is precious; hold on to it.

So you are still here, holding on, and you are still in pain. You are probably asking yourself, "How do I relieve this pain? How can I escape these feelings, even if just for a while?"

Maybe I'll . . .

Get Drunk

Do not drink and drive and do not hurt anyone else while you are drinking, but go ahead get drunk. I would drink a magnum of red wine while lying in my bed and crying myself to sleep. Know that people who are grieving do not turn into happy-go-lucky drunks when they drink. Sooner or later the lack of inhibition gives them permission to become the most obnoxious, self-pitying drunk you have ever seen. It can help you to achieve a near unconscious sleep. But in the morning you will find the pain of your grief is still with you along with the pain of a hangover.

What if I . . .

Take Drugs

Anti-depressants can be very helpful. Your doctor can pre-scribe them. It is like taking out a loan on your grief. Breaking it up into easier-to-handle time payments. Do not be fooled into thinking you will not have to pay off the loan, maybe with interest. Putting off feeling removes the emotion from the event that caused it. This makes the emotion more difficult to under-stand when it does resurface at a later time. If you put off your grief long enough you may need professional help to link your feelings back to the painful event. Listen to your head; listen to your heart, and listen to your doctor.

No No No, I mean . . .

Take Drugs (pot, hash, cocaine, heroin, crack)

This is putting your pain off by flying to never-never land. The pain will still be there when you come down and you will need larger amounts of fairy dust to make each return flight. This is how addictions start and some poor souls never return from never-never land.

How about if I . . .

Eat

Eating until you are very full causes blood to go from your head to your stomach. This is why people often feel sleepy after a large meal. Obviously this has possibilities for one wish-ing to escape. If blood is concentrated in your tummy instead of your head it's harder to have those disturbing thoughts, and if a full tummy makes you feel contented and sleepy, even better. The trouble with this is that if you keep your tummy full all of the time you gain a lot of weight (I gained 25 pounds) during a period when your body is being subjected to a great deal of emotional stress. Go easy.

Okay then, what if I . . .

Don't Eat

This also concentrates one's attention away from the head and heart and makes everything feel empty. Of course you do need food to live.

So leave me alone, I'll just sit and . . .

Watch TV

Turning on the television and leaving it on will numb a mind as well as any anesthetic (home shopping channels work best, but it can be costly).

Hey this is supposed to be boring, and I have tuned into the Lingerie Hour, this makes me think about . . .

Sex (touching and being touched by another human being)

It does help to hold and be held. However, a person in the midst of grief is, by the nature of what they are going through, incapable of giving their full heart to someone new. It is not really fair to take this kind of love when you are in no condition to return it. Your heart is too damaged to share. In time it will heal, become whole and open to love. When the time and the person are right, you will know, but until then go slow.

Will you shut up! You've even managed to make sex sound tedious. I'm going to get into my bed and pull the covers over my head and . . .

Sleep

Putting pajamas on your grief and visiting the sandman is always an option. Sadness like illness is exhausting and sleep if not taken to extremes can be healing. For those of you who have slept on hospital floors and had to dispense medication during the night, sleep might be a healing necessity. It is not unusual for the survivor to collapse from fatigue after the death of their loved one. I laid Debbie's clothes next to me and proceeded to sleep, cry, and deny for two days. It was during that sleep that Debbie's first visitation occurred. I believe that I needed that healing sleep. Know that you can never regain all the sleep you have lost and that disengagement comes at a cost. After a few days it actually hurts to stay in bed, and how could I retreat to a place from which the sick and dying were trying so desperately to escape.

Come to me, all you who are weary and are carrying heavy burdens, and I will give you rest.

Matthew 11:28

Heartwork

chase after a cat
it will run away
quietly work
and it may stay
and wrap its tail
around your toes
but even then
it comes and goes
happiness too
eludes pursuit
heartwork is the artwork
of the absolute
do God's work
and grace so sweet
will curl itself
around your feet

Message on the Bottle

rowing on the burning lake
toward the isle of dreams
swallow deep the firewater
to silence inner screams
numbed heart atrophied
lack of use
loss of need
why whine
wine
drink away
the time and mind
to find the stupid
state of bliss
the surest sign of
cowardice

Message on the Bottle
Black and white acrylic paint on glass
19″ high 19″ in circumference

🍃 8 🍃

GOOD GRIEF

So Mister Smarty Pants, I have been coming up with all of the ideas. Why don't you tell me what does work; what will help; what's your solution?

THE SALINE SOLUTION

when life is a lonely problem
a sad question asking why
there is always
the saline solution
i
feel better after
i
cry

Crying

We as a people are not very good at showing and sharing our emotions. The tides of our tears ebb and flow, but rarely do we allow them to spill over the boundaries of decorum. And so we cry alone. At headstones in graveyards, behind closed doors or hugging the steering wheel of a parked car, in solitude we unleash, weep, wail and talk. We talk to ourselves, to God and most of all we carry on clandestine conversations with the dearly departed. I believe real communication and real healing take place during these tearful talks. After I cried fully and intensely I felt exhausted but also lighter as though a great burden had been lifted from me.

Talking (with family and friends, on the phone, in a bereavement group, with a priest, minister, counselor, or therapist)

You will come to know who your true friends are. They are the ones who will listen to your late night crying. They will invite you to dinner and not care whether you bring the evening to a screeching halt by tearing up at an inappropriate time. (By the

44

way, there is no such time. The time to cry is when you feel like it.) Bereavement groups help by informing you that you are not alone in your pain. The same day that your loved one died, thousands of others also died. The people left behind can help each other. A compassionate counselor, who will listen to you and help you to slowly heal without trying to perform a quick fix, can do wonders. I did all of the above. I accepted every invitation offered, started therapy, talked to a priest and went to a bereavement group. They all helped to keep me going.

Touching and Being Touched

At night I would pile pillows together into the shape of Debbie so that I could sleep in the position I was used to. Pillows do not take the place of people. I had not been touched in six months by anyone beyond a handshake or a quick hug. When animals are left untouched they become depressed and eventually neurotic. It holds true for human beings as well. Get a therapeutic massage. When someone hugs you don't break the embrace so quickly. Put out your hand and hold on for a while. Let yourself be touched.

Heavy Petting

A pet can help pull your attention away from you and your pain, and petting a soft creature who loves and depends on you reduces stress enormously. My little attention grabber and stress reliever is named Trevi, after the famous fountain in Rome. She was named after a fountain because for the first two months she was around she peed on all my worldly possessions. Trevi is a Zen Beagle, all material things are equal in her eyes. These little creatures listen to ancient voices that are only whispers to us. Their instinct to survive and exist in the moment, to fully attend to the sights, scents, and sounds that surround them, speak to an old way of being. Hear the voice of your body. Listen to your whispers.

When I have cried in Trevi's presence she has licked my tears, looked up at me as if to say, "Wouldn't you rather play?" I would; I do.

Moving Your Body, Get Out and About

Just after Debbie died, I did not want to do anything or go anywhere. The places I could think to go, were places that we shared and the things I could think of to do, were things that we did together. I found a sad reminder in every activity. I became aware of the trap I was building for myself on a beautiful summer evening, when a soft breeze fanned the leaves. I looked out the window and thought, "this would be a great time to take a walk."

In the very next moment I also thought, "SHE WALKED."

I began to argue with myself, "That's ridiculous, SHE WALKED, she breathed too, does that mean your breathing reminds you that she's not here."

I answered, "Yes."

"Well you haven't stopped breathing, maybe you can risk a walk, even if it does make you sad."

"Maybe I can!" . . . I did.

Exercising, even just walking, can be an excellent stress reducer. Your body produces chemicals that block pain during sustained exercise. This is going to sound silly, but I love to dance alone in my living room to old soul records. I can't think about anything but the music and rhythm when I dance. It makes me feel better. It makes me feel alive.

Planting and Gardening

Putting seed into soil and watching the fragile stem break ground and stretch out its green neck is an affirmation of and metaphor for life. If you want to grow, you have to stick your neck out. I planted parsley, basil, sunflowers and impatiens. The parsley came up and died within a week. The sunflowers grew incredibly fast and they must have been delicious, because something ate them right down to the ground. The impatiens never came up at all. Ahh, but the basil grew bushy and green and not a leaf was wasted. It made the best pesto that I had ever tasted.

PESTO A LA SMITTY

ONE BUNCH OF FRESH BASIL (about two cups)

ONE Or TWO WHOLE CLOVES OF GARLIC

1/2 CUP OF OLIVE OIL

ONE CUP COARSELY GRATED PARMESAN CHEESE

1/2 CUP PIGNOLI OR PINE NUTS

THREE PLUM TOMATOES

1/2 LEMON

FRESH COARSELY GROUND PEPPER TO TASTE

ONE POUND BOX OF PASTA

Boil water in a large pot. Add a pinch of salt and one teaspoon of olive oil. Place pasta into the pot when water is at a rolling boil. Boil until pasta is al dente' (bites back). Place basil, olive oil, garlic cloves and 1/4 cup of pine nuts into a food processor (this can be done using a mortar and pestle). Process until ingredients are minced in a green sauce. Add parmesan cheese and 1/4 cup of pine nuts to the sauce and pulse the processor to coarsely chop the cheese and pine nuts. Spoon the sauce into a pasta bowl. Drain cooked pasta and place in pasta bowl with sauce. Toss pasta and sauce together using wooden spoon and fork. Squeeze juice of 1/2 lemon into pasta bowl, add three thinly sliced plum tomatoes and pepper to taste. Toss one more time and sprinkle on whole pine nuts and parmesan cheese on top. I suggest that you serve it with a red Zinfandel (Ridge Winery is my favorite) and share it with the people who have helped you the most.

Reading

I read many books during my bereavement. Some of the reading was to help me understand life. Some of it was to help me know I was not alone in the way I was feeling. Some of my readings were an attempt to give substance to the glimpse of the after life that had been given to me. Some of the books I read, especially the clinical ones, did not ring true. I put them down. Other books that I read touched me deeply and helped me. I read them twice. (See my book list on pages 92-94.)

Praying, Meditation, Just Being Still

I think of prayer as talking to God and I found great comfort in those talks. I think of meditation as listening. Meditation opens your mind, body and soul to the healing information in nature and the realm of the spirit. Find a secluded place and allow some stillness in your life.

Creativity (sing, dance, write poetry, paint, sculpt, do needlework)

For me, creativity is my meditation. It has been the most constant and healing of all the measures I have taken. Creative acts bring meaning to the feelings that occur while mourning. I recorded my dreams in a journal, wrote poetry and began painting again. This book is my healing made visible.

Laughing (for crying out loud)

I began this chapter by recommending a good cry and I will end by endorsing a hearty laugh. There truly is nothing funny about death and surely grief can be overwhelming and all encompassing, but I found I became tragically myopic when I allowed loss to be my sole focus. In the periphery, outside the margins of my sadness, lightness and laughter still lived. When I unfixed my gaze and let the light in I was better for it.

For me it meant watching "The Simpsons" or renting the video of Mel Brooks' *Young Frankenstein,* or going to a comedy club. Your beloved did not want you to never smile again. Comedy is, after all, tragedy pushed over the edge. We all have laughed until we cried or cried until we laughed. Exhausting our emotions to their bitter end, until every ounce of sadness is gone may be the only way to clear away enough space to allow absurdity to enter.

At Debbie's memorial service one of the things that served as a pressure release for my welling emotions were the funny stories people told about her. When things got tense at work Debbie was known to say, "I think it's time for a stress pill." Her colleagues' eyebrows would elevate thinking that she was about to take a prescription medication in front them. Laughter would then percolate through the room when she produced a goldfoiled box of chocolate truffles and proceed to pass it around. She was an unashamed chocoholic of the highest degree.

He will wipe away every tear from their eyes. Death will be no more, mourning, and crying and pain will be no more, for the former things have passed away.

Revelation 21:4

Broken Bough
Metamorphosis

broken bough
the
it is here
but
where is the thou
broken heart
dark hollow chest
where do i start
to heal
to fill the empty well
to feel
to grow again and swell
with love inside
the chrysalis
until i break
the painful crust
unfold my wings
and fly with trust
in God

Broken Bough Metamorphosis
Black and white watercolor on rag paper   12″ x 9″

❀ 9 ❀
WOUNDED HEALERS

Commonweal is a place for healing: Healing the individual, healing the family, and healing the planet. Healing is not a one-time fix like a cure, rather it is a recognition of a force within our beings, a spirit that is part of us. Debbie and I went to Commonweal when we had exhausted the options the medical community could offer. When medicine has no cure it offers monitoring and pain relief. These are not little things, but we wanted more. We wanted hope, power and understanding. We needed healing. The Commonweal Cancer Help Program was developed to help people with cancer to discover, understand, feed, strengthen and exercise the healing power in their lives. For one week in a beautiful place, Debbie and I and six other people were asked to change our pattern of living. We were invited to experience: healing touch, healing walk, healing play, healing talk, healing sight, healing food, healing night and healing solitude.

Pacific House

the relentless wind
combs the branches
clinging to the cliffs
wetting them down
like a stubborn cowlick
only to have them
spring up defiantly
when the wind turns its back
inside the pink house
quiet tears wash the walls
shattered dreams
broken parts broken hearts
pieces pieces pieces peace

We are sitting in a casual circle. There are twelve of us: five members of the Commonweal Cancer Help Program staff, seven women with cancer, and me. Michael and Naomi moderate and ask that each person tell their story. He and Naomi begin and are followed by the three other members of the Commonweal team. They have all experienced illness, pain, death and devastating loss. They are wounded healers. Their loss transfigured into compassion, they now share the stories of their journey with us.

Now we are down to the women with cancer and me. We all look at each other hoping someone else will go first. An uncomfortable silence follows.

Then a woman in a bright yellow shirt and a little pink bandanna wrapped around her curly head, spoke: "Well I guess someone has to start, so it might as well be me, my name is Susan."

What bravery, I thought.

What she proceeded to tell us was beautiful and moving. We all cried at different points. She told of a near hopeless diagnosis, insensitive doctors, numerous radiation and chemotherapies, surgeries, despair, depression and anger. She ended with a very simple story about finding a dead owl on the side of the road. She believed the event to be a sign that she would survive. She has survived for many years now. I was so impressed by her and her telling of the event; I wrote the poem and painted the painting that follows.

The Owl

death had already
lifted your soul
when i saw your eyes glow
from the side of the road

i stopped
turned the truck
drawn back to your side
what owl gift
did your owl eyes hide

i laid your body down
on the truck's steel bed
a hard metal pillow
for a soft feathered head

on the road
on my way once again
i came to the place
where i would have been
death was there
cars had crashed
fire smoke and broken glass

what owl gift
did your owl eyes hide
another night passed
and i did not die

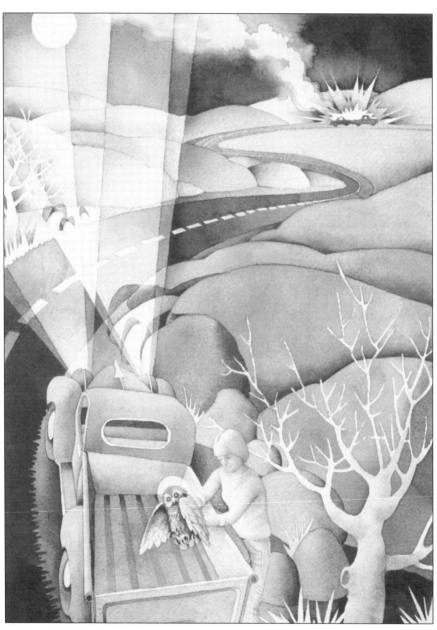

The Owl
Black and white watercolor on rag   12″ x 9″

❧ 10 ❧

WOUNDED HEALERS (continued)

One by one the women tell the stories of their lives and their cancers. A lump in the breast that requires a mastectomy, lung cancer, Crohn's disease with intestinal cancer, chronic mylogenic leukemia, an inoperable brain tumor being treated by radiation, and then it is Debbie's turn.

Debbie, with poise and grace, unfolds the story of her life, our relationship, her remarkable career, and then she begins to draw a verbal diagram of her disease. The clinical name is Mylodisplatic syndrome, aplastic anemia, mylofibrosis pro-acute leukemia. She had a nearly complete bone marrow failure. Doctors seven months earlier had given her two to six months to live. Hers was the lone terminal diagnosis in the room. No percentages were ever offered by the doctors she saw, just that she might be wise to get her affairs in order.

She already felt triumphant by outliving their death sentence prediction by a month. She was defiantly determined to fight with every atom of her body to live, and she did live for nine more months. Her power and eloquence were remarkable.

I dissolved into a weeping mass of emotion. I had hoped that I might be exempted. I was not. It was my turn to speak. I briefly told the story of my life. As I concluded I looked around the room and realized that this evening had been one of the most significant in the life I had just summarized. We, these women, Michael and myself had truly become one person, shared one soul, felt perfect empathy. There was a hum in the air and the room seemed to be lit by the bodies of the people around me. I closed by saying that I was honored to be in the same room with them. I had never experienced the level of honesty and compassion that radiated in that place, in that holy space. Somehow, truth and pain had made them great.

I was reminded of what the photographer Dianne Arbus had said when she was asked why she photographed people who were deformed, social outcasts or diseased. Her answer inspired the following.

Thank You Dianne

why do you photograph
dwarfs giants and hermaphrodites
these are pitiful people
it is simply not right

we wait all our lives
dreading possible disaster
insuring ourselves
against the hand of the master
side stepping
avoiding
the inevitable pain
taking few chances
playing safe at the game
uneasy we see them
unconscious we stare
life will eventually
deliver us there
freaks
born with the tragedy
accidents at birth
surviving examples
of pain here on earth
when your body fails
when you sit where they sat
their status is unveiled
each one
an aristocrat

❧ 11 ❧

HEROES ARE HUMANS

there are times when it is difficult to see god
in the faces of our fellow travelers on earth
the journey wrinkles us and throws up dust
on the road to death from birth
but o sweet friend there are moments
when i see God in you
when angel light and all that is right
burst forth and come shining through
thank you for all the love you gave
for all the love you still send
for showing me that heroes are just humans
good family, good neighbors and good friends

The heroes in my life are just humans like you and me. Ordinary people, who act with compassion and courage, become heroic. By compassion I mean a simple kindness. By courage I mean pushing past fear and doing what our hearts tell us to do. Foremost among my heroes is Debbie.

She suffered so much pain with such incredible dignity and strength. She loved life and never stopped fighting to live. Five months before she died she was sitting in a hospital being transfused and she decided she wanted to give a party to celebrate the miracle of life. She said "If I do live, now is the time I need my friends most, and if I don't live I want to say goodbye to the people I love." The party date was set. The invitation read:

Come celebrate the joy of life.

Let us eat, drink and be merry.

Your laughter, tears and vigilant

watch have strengthened me.

The power of love is a mighty force.

United in one place and time

perhaps we will spark a miracle.

If you are unable to join us

remember us on October 28th

as we will toast our friends

near and far.

October 28th came and Debbie was experiencing severe bone pain. I had to help her manage the few steps from the bed to the bathroom. Friends had flown in from all over the country. I wanted to cancel the party. Debbie told me that if I did she would never speak to me again. That afternoon Debbie's mother and I helped her bathe. I dried her hair and I rolled a large comfortable office chair into the bathroom so that she could do her make-up one step at a time. We helped her put on a new red sequined dress that she had purchased for the evening. I looked at her and was astonished to see that she had transformed herself from sick to stunning. She looked absolutely beautiful (miracle #1).

Party time came around and Mom and I each took an arm and led Debbie to the hall we had rented for the occasion. When we got to the door Debbie pulled her arms away from us and with a great effort straightened up and entered the room under her own power (miracle #2).

Everyone in the hall stood and cheered. People left their chairs and gathered round to greet and hug her. She took a seat and began to receive people like a princess at court.

People said to me, "She looks terrific, you would never know she was sick."

We had dinner and our friends had prepared entertainment for us, a magic act, a hula dance, beautiful singing and music. As the evening passed I noticed that Debbie was not tiring, quite to the contrary she seemed to be gathering momentum. She began standing more and moving about the room (miracle #3).

We had hired a disc jockey to provide dance music and we had picked out all of our favorite oldies for him to play. He had set up speakers and a microphone and was about to begin the music. Just then Debbie came to me and said, "I want to say something to everybody, would you get me the microphone."

I brought it to her, she took it into her hand and walked to the center of the room and said, "Thank you all for coming here tonight and special thanks to those who have flown or driven long distances to be here. I love you all. I want to thank you for your cards, letters and phone calls; they help, they keep me going. Thank you also to all of you who have visited me in the hospital and a special thanks to all who have donated blood in my name. Without it I would not be here tonight. I feel uplifted by the love in this room, as though your loving eyes were holding me and supporting me. What the doctors say does not sound too promising. But if I believed everything doctors said I would not be alive tonight. There is hope. We are starting some new experimental therapies and who knows, a miracle could happen. I would like to make a toast, to friends near and far, to love, to miracles and to life." Everyone stood and cheered, the disc jockey played the song "Lady in Red" and I dissolved into tears. Debbie came over to me and said, "let's dance, Smitty" (miracle #4).

For three more hours she danced nearly every dance. At the end of the evening everyone gathered into a circle and we played the song "That's What Friends Are For." We all cried and gathered up the ribbon-tied, helium-filled balloons that were all around the room and went outside, where we saw above us the most incredible starry sky. We let the balloons go all at once and as our eyes followed them upward a shooting star etched an arc across the heavens. Thank you, God (miracle #5).

The Gazelle

a gazelle
grace in movement
grace in form
became aware of the lion

thought of running

but then turned and
faced the devouring force

the lion stopped
surprised and confused
can it be that she
will fight me?

the gazelle
braced its forelegs
lowered head and horn
and fenced with the lion's claw
and parried each thrust
of the lion's paw
with horn so smooth
and sharp and shear
the cat barely knew
that its fur had been pierced

the lion retreated
and looked from side to side
to see if the battle
had been observed

embarrassed that this creature
of light and grace
had turned and fought him
face to face
and won

the lion wondered
had other gazelles seen
might they learn not to flee
could they lose their fear of me

the lion looked back
at the gazelle
and fell in love
how could he not
with her beauty and strength
and the way that she fought
but he also knew
that she must be killed
he could not have gazelles
being so strong willed

the lion stalked her
and waited until
her heel was bruised
and when she tripped and fell
the lion took her from behind

too weakened
to defend
the gazelle
looked at the lion
and said
you have my body
but not my spirit
and the other
gazelles have seen
that you fear it
my body will go to grass
and feed their fawn
and when they fight back
it will be me going on

The Gazelle
Black and white watercolor on rag paper   12″ x 9″

🎄 12 🎄

WHY ARE WE HERE AND
WHERE ARE WE GOING?

No one truly knows the answers to these questions. These are only my opinions, substantiated only by visions and personal experience. When we ask these questions, we are left with our faith and very little evidence. Your beliefs are most likely different from mine. If your belief supports you in your grief, if it fortifies you against the pain, if it adds peace and understanding to the meaning of your loss, your belief—your religion—is fulfilling its purpose.

Like the peaks of little waves shimmering in the moonlight we are individuals, catching and reflecting light, and yet, it is one light that we reflect and one ocean of which we are a part. We are here to experience life and then learn and grow from that experience. Life is about cycles and time. The cycle of coming into being and dying. It is the experience of death in our own lives that awakens an awareness of death, dying and loss in the lives of others. This is the awareness of oneness. This is the birth of compassion. This is the awakening of love. We are here to learn this.

In this life God reserves the power of intervention for himself and uses that power with great restraint, for if God were to rescue us from every travail and every problem it would surely subvert our free will and stunt our growth, even as it does with children who are overprotected and overindulged. I believe God allows the souls of our departed loved ones to exert some small influence on our lives. They give us gentle nudges, pats on the back and sometimes kicks in the behind.

I found after Debbie's death that I could look into someone's eyes and know whether they had experienced the death of a loved one. I began to call them "the initiated." Not everyone gets the lesson. Some experience loss and become bitter and

64

angry, others simply withdraw from participation in life. There are also those wonderful creatures that are born with their hearts wide open and full of compassion and have no need of further experience. We are blessed by their presence.

Why do we react so differently? Some people are only beginning their life studies, while others are taking their final exams just before graduation. God made us in the image of God. The Final Examination involves seeing that image in you and in every person and in every creature and in every plant and in the earth and in the stars. Graduation is treating everyone and everything as you would treat God, as you would treat yourself.

This is the vision that is delivered to every person at the time of his or her death. The light that is seen by people who have returned from near death experiences is, I believe, our welcome home party. As our spirit returns to spirit it is embraced by the radiance of many souls glowing with perfect compassion, perfect knowledge and perfect love. They are connected by a lace work of love and light. This lace work is sometimes called the net of Indra, or the web of life and light, or Jacob's ladder, or the heavenly host, or the face of God.

The kingdom of the Father will not come by expectation. The kingdom of the Father is spread upon the earth and men do not see it.

Gnostic Gospel According to St. Thomas

❧ 13 ☙

THE ETERNAL CITY
(A DREAM)

Debbie and I are entering the Colosseum in Rome (the eternal city). The Colosseum is restored to its ancient glory or should I say gory, for in this open-air theater humans choreographed some of the bloodiest and most horrific entertainments ever conceived of. We are in the very top row of seats. An usher in a black tuxedo comes to me and says, "You are wanted on stage." On stage a bloody ballet is being performed. Gladiators and wild animals are tearing each other apart. The sand beneath them is soaked red. I say that I do not want to go down there. The usher says, "You must." I say that I do not want to leave Debbie. Debbie says, "You must." So I walk down the many steps to the stage. When I step on the stage all of the fighting has ceased and instead of animals and warriors doing battle there is an orchestra. I look up into the Colosseum seats and I see thousands of lights, but I cannot see Debbie. I ask the conductor of the orchestra why I cannot see her. He says, "The lights prevents you from seeing the audience from the stage." I look up again and the individual lights merge into one light. This light is blinding. I shield my eyes and I ask the orchestra conductor, "If you cannot see the audience how do you know they are up there?"

The conductor responds, "We feel their pity when we perform poorly; it is compassion for us; it is the voice of our conscience, and we hear their applause and feel the breeze from their blown kisses when we play well together; it is joy; it is bliss."

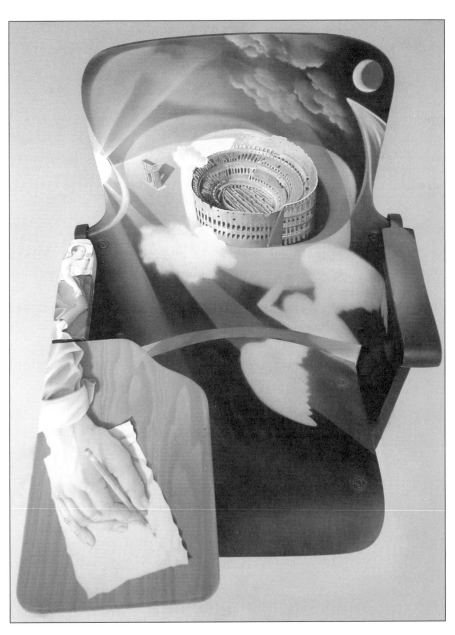

Seat of the Soul
Black and white oil paint on lecture hall chair   40″ x 28″

Mourning Sickness

mourning sickness
growth and change
dance this dance
with
loss and pain
see the furred petaled and winged world
eating destroying being born and unfurled
searing fearful horrific and blind
peaceful potent serene and sublime
testing testing
are you prepared to conceive
to deal with
what is dealt
from the magician's sleeve
you are pregnant with God
you are great with soul
giving birth to yourself
is life's greatest goal
do not be stillborn again

Mourning Sickness
Black and white watercolor on rag paper   12″ x 9″

Stream of Consciousness

drop

of

water

tiny puddle
drop of water
little stream
drop of water
mighty river
raging torrent
of human dreams
ceaseless filling spilling flow
dew and rain and melting snow
swell steadily toward the ocean end
where all of our souls will touch and blend
synapse in the almighty mind
vision past the fog of time
beyond the fiery wall of fear
and comprehend the cosmic
tear

❦ 14 ❦
THE PROUD WOUND

The grief hole in your chest is a spiritual wound. If this wound were in your skin, your flesh, doctors would call it a Proud Wound. No suture, no stitch will close such a lesion. The wound must be left open and allowed to heal from the perimeter inward. Adding small amounts of tissue each day, the body rebuilds the injured flesh cell by cell. This process is called granulation. Over a period of weeks and months the walls of the wound close. Day by day the process is impossible to perceive, but measured weekly and monthly the hole slowly closes. Infection from outside entities may impede the progress. The wound may weep uncontrollably. If the patient moves quickly, or too much, the delicate new tissue may reopen at the edges. Eventually the wound closes. Some parts of the scar tissue are raw, red and tender (hypersensitive), other areas are numb with no feeling at all. In time this scar tissue becomes more and more like the normal skin that surrounds it, but it will always remain distinct. It will always be a scar no matter how complete the healing. The body will always carry the memory of the wound. From hole to whole the body heals.

Allow your spiritual body the time and stillness it needs to heal.
You will be whole again.

Miss Tree

the
sign said
come and see
the drive-thru tree
in my mind eye pictured
a behemoth standing dead
chainsaw gutted
by a brainless biped
she tugged on my sleeve
and said please let's drive through it
i said what the hell
and turned the car to it
down a winding dirt road
in a forest of redwood
the rented car drove
to drive through the dead wood
two dollars per auto
was the price for the sight
i pulled Chrysler in
and looked up with delight
the giant had been struck by lightning
and hollowed by fire
but it was alive
and stood to inspire
two thousand years
of struggle and strife
this tree had lived
one hell of a life
burned out and scarred
the tree lived and it grew

so can i
so can you

Miss Tree
Black and white watercolor on rag paper   12″ x 9″

❧ 15 ❧
NOBODY KNOWS THE TROUBLE I'VE SEEN
(A teeny tiny play in one act)

CHARACTERS

Keith - *The guy writing this book, wife died from leukemia, grieving and book are nearly complete.*

Gino - *A first generation Italian-American, owner of a restaurant, grieving the death of his only son, the boy nineteen years of age, died six months earlier in a car crash while driving under the influence of alcohol.*

Arie - *Artist, university professor, a first generation Jewish-American, survivor of the Holocaust, lost aunts, uncles and cousins in concentration camps, younger brother died of starvation and five-year-old sister died in 1941 in a work camp in the Ural Mountains, only natural son miscarried in the fourth month of wife's pregnancy, father died when Arie was twenty-five, friend to both Gino and Keith.*

ACT ONE

SCENE I

A little Italian restaurant, Arie and Keith are sitting, Gino the owner approaches the table.

Arie: *(whispers to Keith)*
This is the owner of the restaurant coming towards us.

Keith: *(whispers to Arie)*
Is he the one that lost his son in the car accident?

Arie: Yes, that's him.

Gino arrives at the table looking very sad.

Arie: Hello Gino.

Gino: Hello Arie.

Arie and Gino shake hands.

Arie: Gino this is Keith; Keith, Gino

Keith and Gino shake hands.

Keith: It's a pleasure to meet you Gino.

Gino shakes his head yes.

Arie: So, how are you doing?

Gino shakes his head no.

Gino: Terrible. Nobody knows.

Keith: Arie told me about your son. I'm very sorry.
This is a very tough time you're going through.
I lost my wife two years ago.

Gino looks up sharply.

Gino: A wife! A wife is not the same!
A son is blood of your blood!
You can't know, nobody knows.

Arie: Yes, you're right Gino, nobody knows the trouble
you've seen.
How is your wife doing?

Gino rolls his eyes upward and shrugs.

Gino: She doesn't understand, you know how women are
. . . Crazy.

THE END

🐚 16 🐚

THE PAIN GAME

I do not know why this happens, but it does. It has happened to me too many times to not speak about it. Some people seem to want to devalue your pain and inflate their pain to the point that no human could possibly empathize with them. No one could have experienced the level of their loss and the depths of their pain. In the history of humanity, in the annals of time they are unique and alone in the grandeur of their suffering, and in a way they are right. Nobody has lived a life exactly like theirs. No one has loved the person they lost in precisely the same way they did. Their pain and the magnitude of their loss is incomprehensible to them, how could anyone else understand it. How could anyone in the past have felt this badly and they not be aware of it? That would make them incredibly insensitive, almost unconscious not to have noticed a pain such as theirs preexisting in the world. No, it must be that their pain is a new species, an unprecedented and monstrous mutation that sprang from the loins of their loss. They are inconsolable. Feed them, shelter them, listen to them and love them, but do not suggest that you know how they feel. They are separate and alone.

I believe in the first weeks of grieving this is a natural state of being. But if you persist in perceiving yourself as separate from nature, apart from other people and scorned by God, you will not heal. I have been told that my loss was less significant than the loss of a child, the loss of a parent, the loss of a husband, the loss of a lover, the loss of a marriage, the loss of being dumped by a girlfriend and the loss of a pet. In the early days of my mourning, when I also thought that my pain was > greater than theirs and > greater than anybody's, these people would piss me off royally. A dead dog, for God's sake. I now believe that their pain was not < less than, but = equal to mine. Pain is pain. Loss is loss. The depth of grief is not measured by marriage or relative relationship, by birth or species membership, but by the depth of love given to and received from that which was lost. All who live are qualified to love. All who love are qualified to mourn. All who mourn are worthy of your compassion. The pain game is always a tie.

Lesson Loss

the landscape of loss
mountains to climb
canyons to cross
callused skin
hallowed heart
when you fall
is when you start
the open wound lets light in
the light gives strength
you stand again
light in exchange
for aching pain
lessen loss
lessen gain

"If you have made mistakes, there is always another chance for you. You may have a fresh start any moment you choose, for this thing we call 'failure' is not the falling down, but the staying down."   —Mary Pickford

🏵. 17 🏵

NATURAL DISASTER

In the process of trying to heal Debbie, healing myself, and endeavoring to pass on what I learned to help others to heal, I became very aware of the damage we are inflicting on the earth. When you realize your oneness with other people, it leads to an understanding of your oneness with nature, and the earth and all of the creatures and processes of the earth. My loss sensitized me to loss in general. Nowhere is loss more profoundly manifest than in the purity of the air, clarity of the water, quality of the soil and health of the plant and animal communities. The cancers in our bodies are testaments to the fouling of these systems.

Species go extinct when they do not adapt to change. Things that hinder adaptation are overspecialization, overpopulation, overornamentation and overarmoring. By these criteria we humans are certainly candidates for the endangered species list. Watching nature and its processes was a large part of my healing. How will we heal, when the processes we observe in nature fail? I believe we, as a species must evolve from parasitic (an entity that consumes its host) to symbiotic creatures (an entity which consumes but also restores, fortifies or gives back to the host).

The earth is our host. We have been poor guests. The earth's future hospitality depends on our manners. The earth's systems are much larger and more powerful than our invented human systems. Witness the chaos when the earth shivers—an earthquake—our cities crumble; when she coughs—a hurricane—our houses tumble; when she cries—a flood—levies fail and turn to mud. How strange it is that in these moments of crisis we treat each other as brother and as sister. The ego-shattering, future-crushing aspects of a natural disaster bring forth the awareness of how tenuous and fragile our lives are and that under our jobs, our clothes, our skins we are alike.

100% Recycled

every molecule
every atom
every particle
of mine
is recycled stuff
from the beginning of time
my baggage is stacked
on a spiral stair
all of my things
are organized there
as a house full of boxes
on moving day
this body is packed with my DNA
my current address
is a human being
but
rearrange the chairs
and i am a finch's wing
interior decorate
and i am a graceful gazelle
or a shining pine needle
or a whelk in its shell
wherever i go
and whatever i see
i find that
i am finding
little particles
of me

A day will come when you realize that twenty-four hours have passed and you have not cried. You might even feel a little guilty about it. A day will come when you realize that you are laughing out loud and that it feels good and that it is okay to laugh again.

The Backpack

as i walked through the days of my mourning
following the path of my grief
i carried a heavy backpack filled with sad stones
the weight of my loss the wait of my loss
it bent me over it cast my eyes down
each day a sad stone was added
the weight the wait became so great
some days i could not walk
some days i could not stand
the slow cool hand of God
reached down without my knowing
and took a sad stone
and the weight stopped growing
with each step i took
God took a stone
stepping stone stepping stone
i thought that i was completely alone
until the weight was lessened
waiting lesson patience path
each sad stone paved a step
each step created the path the way
day by day the pack became light
steps became light
Life became light
God finally took away all of the sad stones
my pack was empty but i had grown
the weight the wait had made my back strong
but without the sad stones how do i go on?

how do i remember my sorrow and her death?
she whispered to me with her divine breath
fill your pack with a blanket a bottle and some bread
there is someone to love she waits just ahead
and remember me living and not just my dying
i liked picnics much more than crying

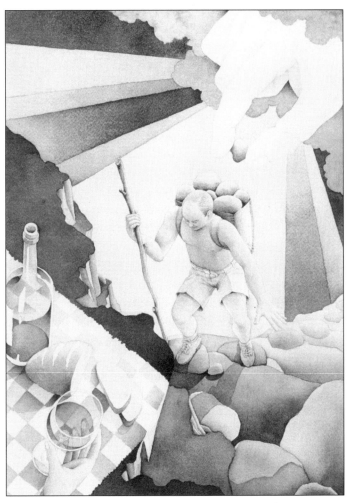

The Backpack
Black and white watercolor on rag paper   12″ x 9″

❦ 18 ❦
THE BOY

My mourning sickness lasted two years. I am still the keeper of the soul. Time expands between the tears. The hole in me is now whole. The deep pain is gone. My proud wound is a scar. When I think of Debbie now it is as often with a smile at a remembered joy as it is a tear at a remembered pain. I do not think I am meant to forget the pain. I am branded by it. It is part of the architecture of my life.

When a Roman general returned to the eternal city after a victorious battle, the citizens of Rome would line the streets, cheering and throwing flower petals into his path. Riding in a golden chariot the general would lead his troops dressed in their finest armor, with victory banners and battle flags streaming in the wind. Standing next to the general in the chariot was a small servant boy. As the crowd chanted the name of the conquering hero the boy would whisper into the general's ear "Remember thou art mortal."

My pain, my loss, is that boy. He was once a giant. He was once my master. Pain would say cry now and I would cry, and loss would lash my heart until it bled. I tried to run away. He would find me and beat me all the harder for attempting the escape. After many months a strange thing happened; I began to grow and he began to shrink, until finally he became a small boy. Now, he is my faithful servant. When my head fills with pride, he says, "Remember how she died." When I am mean to a stranger or I criticize a friend, he says, "Remember, remember this life will end." When I fail to notice the incredible beauty of this earth, or to live life with gratitude and joy, I feel a tap on my shoulder, look down and there is the boy, whispering . . .

"Remember thou art mortal."

Hymn to Her

crocus bow your head
beneath the crusted snow
frozen meditation
icy preparation
of one who is about to grow
frost on velvet lips
cold and silent prayer
syllables once spoken
hang cloudly in the air
melting the despair
unchilling chambers of the
heart
i thought no longer there
auricle
oracle
open up and flower
mirror blue the sky
let go let glow
your sunny center
open your third eye
ventricle
vent trickle

stillness thaws
and becomes fluidity
filling every volume
greening every tree
branches motion to the
winged
here a home here a perch
lake and river fully thinged
there a spawning there a
birth
the curving of her body
the swelling of her breast
the flowering of her valley
the scent of her sweet breath
her to him
the living limb
him to her
the healing the cure
hymn to her
endear
endure

❦ 19 ❦
TOUCHING THE ETERNAL

We put our hands together when we pray. In this gesture we close the circle of our arms and approach the divine. The coming together of our bodies in making love can also be a prayer. The laces of love entwine and we merge. The solitary urge becomes two combined. This sweet combination expands and gives birth to a third way of being that is not of this earth. The body parts subside. The swelling hearts imbibe the ambrosia of eternity. Overtaken by the sense of you being me and I being we and we being everything. Until the moment when awareness of self and time is completely destroyed. You float above your body, you sail over joy...

Then the world seeps in, thoughts flood the void and soon you must swim just to stay buoyed. The weight of your body and awareness of time and life return. The sweet exhaustion, the hot afterburn of this carbon base, earthen vase. We splash down, still clinging to the memory of innerspace.

I believe that in these tender shared moments we do touch the eternal. We taste pure love, and life becomes transparent to the transcendent. We break through physical reality and experience the world of the soul, in other words, we hit one out of the park and the glorious moment in the sun is fleeting. These transcendent moments are happening all the time. They occur at births and deaths and during walks in the woods and wherever people come together with a spirit of true compassion leading their hearts. It can happen at a wedding, an AA meeting, a bereavement group, a high school reunion, or a Girl Scout troop. A glow fills the room and light fills the space, and love fills our hearts and we touch God's face.

Rush in Roulette

while you are busy planning
adding to your
trust fund
your life is busy spanning
loading up
a gun
careful
you do not know
how much you risk
prudence
trading precious moments
for the hope of future bliss
now
is the time
for heavy petting
get sweaty back seat kissed
now
is the time
to make love to your life
to aim elsewhere is to have
missed
add to your
trust of fun
live

NOW and NOW
again
tomorrow will be
NOW
soon enough
and today will soon be then

while watching the movie
Zorba the Greek
it seemed so sad and pro-
found
i looked at the cuteness next
to me
and noticed that she frowned
she said
Zorba would not watch this
movie
he would make love and
dance

spin the chamber of the gun
trigger
CLICK
another chance!

Heliotrope

the leaf unfolds
opens
turns to the warmth
bends toward the light
leans to the love
knows that it's right

resolve to revolve

the leaf grows
absorbs
and takes the light in
at one with the light
at one with the wind
loose of the limb
freedom flag
of amber and red
wave your fire branded head

cherubim

affinity to divinity
resolve to dissolve
time to feed

a seed

Two Lips and Tulips
Black and white oil painting on canvas   48″ x 32″

❧ 20 ❧

ONE AND ONLY
(Soul Mates)

I fell in love with Debbie when I was fourteen years old. I can vividly remember the moment. It was at one of those uneasy adolescent parties your parents drive you to, and other parents rightfully over-chaperone. Debbie was beautiful, intelligent and full of grace. I fell foot-in-my-mouth, full-out-foolish in love with her. I pursued her and wooed her until three years later she decided that maybe she was in love with me.

After that we dated steadily for five years and were married at the age of twenty-one. During the next fifteen years there were many wonderful moments, but also times of tension, times of anger and times we disappointed each other. Through all of those times, I knew she loved me; she knew I loved her, and we both knew that our love would endure.

When Debbie died I had never been with another woman. I do not tell you this because I think that is the way it should be or to impress you with my moral fiber, but to help you understand how terrified I was at the thought of approaching another woman. I did not think I would ever love again. I had deep doubts about whether I could function sexually with another woman. I feared no one would want a man so damaged, and I also feared I would be alone the rest of my life. If I were to have put an honest personal ad in the paper it would have read like this:

> Male, tall, overweight, nearly bald, very limited sexual experience, heart broken. Wishes to meet beautiful, intelligent, understanding, and patient woman. Object to fill overwhelming void in life.

Amazingly enough there were women who applied. I began dating and met several wonderful women who fulfilled all the criteria of the preceding ad. I also found that I was capable of caring again.

It was about two years A.D.D. (After Debbie's Death) that I met Ginny. It was not love at first sight, nor did I immediately fall head over heals, but slowly, beautifully, totally and completely I came to love her. She is the "she" in Yes Dear the last poem in this book. She loves to drive through trees, and she is the one who thinks Zorba would not waste his time watching his own movie when he could be dancing. And she is the one who has helped to bring color, light and love back into my life. My hymn is to her.

I am sharing this only to point out that if there was anyone who believed in the idea of soul mates, love at first sight and a one-and-only, once-in-a-life time love, it was I. Now I believe that the love we are capable of is deeper and wider than we can imagine. We can focus and bring wonderful love to any number of deserving people in our lives, but the ultimate goal that God wishes for us and that life is designed to teach, is that we are meant to love and respect every person, every living thing, and indeed the whole wonderful world.

We are miracles after all.

Yes Dear

I said, "Why are we here?"
she sipped on a beer.
"What does it all mean?"
she licked the ice cream.
"Why must we die?"
she chased a butterfly.
"Is our life just chance?"
she laughed and she danced.
"Does God exist?"
she hugged me and kissed.
"Is there a heaven above?"
she said, "Let's make love."
I said, "Heaven's right here!"

She said, "Yes dear, yes dear."

In the eternal city of Rome,
at the Colosseum
I asked Ginny to marry me . . .

She said, "Yes dear."

MY BOOK LIST

This is a list of the books that were helpful to me.

The Holy Bible

All of **M. Scott Peck**'s books are important and well worth reading. My favorites are:

Further Along the Road Less Traveled
Simon and Schuster, New York, NY 1993.
Other than the Bible, the most truthful guidebook to earthly and spiritual life I have read.

In Search of Stones
Hyperion Inc., New York, NY 1995.
Part travel guide and part life guide, this book is a wonderful read with beautiful terra cotta illustrations.

People of the Lie
Simon and Schuster, New York, NY, 1983.
An essential read for anyone who has to deal with someone they consider to be evil.

A World Waiting to Be Born
Bantam Doubleday Dell Publishing Group, Inc., New York, NY, 1993.
Presents a way of being that if embraced has the potential to bring healing and peace to the world.

Anything written by **Joseph Campbell** is worth a read. My favorites are:

The Hero With a Thousand Faces
Princeton University Press, Princeton, NJ, 1949.
The hero's journey as described in stories, myths, and parables throughout the ages is a quest that each of us embarks upon at the moment of our birth.

The Power of Myth
Joseph Campbell interviewed by Bill Moyers
Bantam Doubleday Dell Publishing Group, Inc., New York, NY, 1988.
I also highly recommend the viewing of this six-part video series.

Animals As Teachers and Healers
Susan Chernak McElroy
Ballantine Publishing Group, Random House Inc., New York, NY, 1997.
A touching and beautiful book for anyone who has lost a beloved pet or felt the healing power in being close to nature.

Barefoot on Holy Ground
Gloria Karpinski
Balantine Publishing Group, Random House, Inc., New York, NY, 2001.
Presents twelve lessons with accompanying exercises in spiritual craftsmanship.

Black Elk Speaks
Nicolas Black Elk and John G. Neihardt
William Morrow and Company, New York, NY, 1932.
The narrative of a spiritual journey taken by a young boy who is given a vision to bring back to his people. I recommend reading Hero With A Thousand Faces *before reading* Black Elk Speaks.

Choices in Healing
Michael A. Lerner
MIT Press, Cambridge, MA, 1994.
A book about the integration of the best conventional and complementary medicine.

Creative Healing
Michael Samuels and Mary R. Lane
HarperCollins Publishers, Inc., New York, NY, 1998.
This book is about how to use art as a healing force.

Drawing on the Right Side of the Brain
Betty Edwards
Penguin Putnam, Inc., New York, NY, 1989.
If you want to learn how to draw what you see and feel, do the exercises in this book while you read it.

Healing and the Mind
Bill Moyers
Bantam Doubleday Dell Publishing Group, Inc., New York,
NY, 1993.
*Reveals how profoundly our minds and spirits affect the phys-
ical health of our bodies.*

Healing Words
Larry Dossey
Harper Collins, New York, NY, 1993.
*Brings to light a significant body of empirical data that strongly
supports the efficacy of prayer in healing.*

Life After Life
Raymond A. Moody
Bantam Doubleday Dell Publishing Group, Inc., New York,
NY, 1976.
*Examines more than one hundred case studies of people who
were pronounced dead and later were revived. Their stories
have a remarkable similarity and offer a glimpse of the peace
and love that await us on the other side of this life.*

The Mythic Imagination
Stephen Larsen
Bantam Doubleday Dell Publishing Group, Inc., New York,
NY, 1990.
*Helps the layperson recognize, understand and use the mythic
adventures each of us are living out in our daily lives.*

On Death and Dying
Elizabeth Kubler-Ross
Macmillan, New York, NY, 1969.
*A groundbreaking book that explores the feelings of people
who have been given a terminal diagnosis.*

For further information about Keith Smith's artwork or to
arrange a speaking engagement:

ksmith@ccm.edu
awakenmysoul.com

Healing Resources from Resurrection Press

MEDITATIONS FOR SURVIVORS OF SUICIDE
Joni Woelfel

". . . leaves us with a conviction that survivors of suicide can truly live again with courage, hope and a new resurrection."
—Antoinette Bosco

". . . an accessible and truly comforting book. I wholeheartedly recommend this inspiring resource for anyone surviving the suicide of a loved one, or indeed for anyone who grieves."
—Amy Florian, Liturgy and Bereavement Consultant

No. RP 170/04 ISBN 1-878718-75-4　　　　**Price: $8.95**

HEALING YOUR GRIEF
Sr. Ruthann Williams, O.P.

"Sr. Ruthann . . . shares her insights as to what to say and be in the midst of death and what not to say and not to be."
—Msgr. Thomas Hartman

No. RP 530/04 ISBN 1-878718-29-0　　　**Price: $7.95**

HEART PEACE
Embracing Life's Adversities
Adolfo Quezada

"This is one of the most authentic books I have ever read on the gut wrenching conditions that cause or lead to human suffering. . . . His book is a gift, allowing others to be the beneficiaries of his spiritual journey."
—Antoinette Bosco

No. RP 117/04 ISBN 1-878718-52-5　　　**Price: $9.95**

MOTHER O' MINE: A Legacy of Remembrance
Harry W. Paige

Rich in imagery, history and spirituality, these stories evoke the nearness of those we have loved—beyond the graves that hold them. A perfect gift for anyone who has or desires a deep and abiding love for their mother.

"Harry Paige has been a favorite of Catholic Digest readers for more than four decades. This evocative collection in honor of his mother makes it easy to see why."
—Richard Reece, Editor

No. RP 182/04 ISBN 1-878718-81-9　　　　**Price: $9.95**

www.catholicbookpublishing.com

Additional Titles Published by Resurrection Press, a Catholic Book Publishing Imprint

For a free catalog call 1-800-892-6657
www.catholicbookpublishing.com